A.N. BART
HOME MAINTENANCE

The Ultimate Guide on How to Become Your Very Own Handyman, Learn DIY Tips and Become a Professional Repair Expert in No Time

Descrierea CIP a Bibliotecii Naționale a României
A.N. BART
    HOME MAINTENANCE. The Ultimate Guide on How to Become Your Very Own Handyman, Learn DIY Tips and Become a Professional Repair Expert in No Time / A.N. Bart – Bucharest: Editura My Ebook, 2021
    ISBN

A.N. BART

HOME MAINTENANCE
The Ultimate Guide on How to Become Your Very Own Handyman, Learn DIY Tips and Become a Professional Repair Expert in No Time

My Ebook Publishing House
Bucharest, 2021

TABLE OF CONTENTS

Introduction 7

Chapter 1: *Essential Tools For A Professional Handyman* 9

Chapter 2: *Top Skills 1: Woodworking* 13

Chapter 3: *Top Skills 2: Plumbing* 16

Chapter 4: *Top Skills 3: Basic Electronics* 19

Chapter 5: *Top Skills 4: Advanced Electronics* 22

Chapter 6: *Working On Floors, Walls & Ceilings* 25

Chapter 7: *Working On Windows, Doors & Lighting* ... 28

Chapter 8: *Working On Bathrooms, Kitchens & Basements* 31

Chapter 9: *Working On The House Exterior* ………….. 34

Chapter 10: *Protect Yourself From Injuries* ………….. 37

Chapter 11: *Always Have A First Aid Kit* ……………. 40

Wrapping Up ………………………………………….. 43

INTRODUCTION

There is usually a set style of tools that is suitable for anyone wanting to be a handyman. When it comes to having the right handyman tools, getting a set with some level of quality is better than just throwing together a few bit and pieces to make up a kit. This is quite basic and should be very easy to acquire.

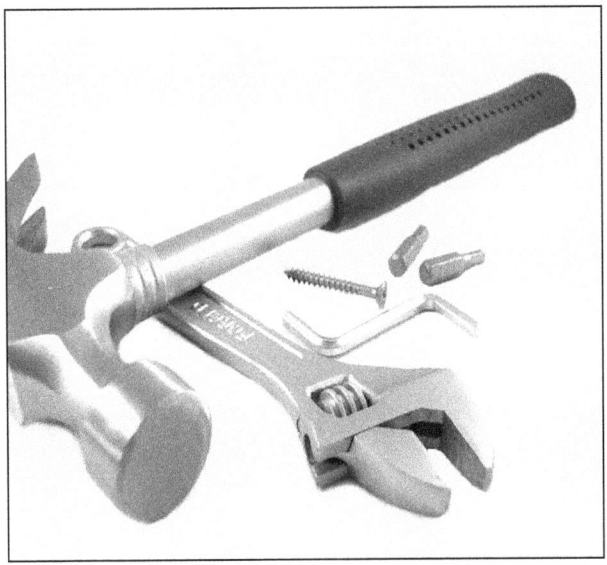

Chapter 1

Essential Tools For A Professional Handyman

Synopsis

Good tools can make the difference between a well done and easy experience and a frustrating and poorly finished job. This is one of the secrets of a good handyman, as matching the correct tools to the job is part of getting the best results and an overall satisfying experience.

The Basic Tools

The following are some of the tools that should be part of the tool kit of a professional handyman:

• *16 0z claw hammer* – this is suitable for medium weight hammering jobs. However, if needed, a lighter or heavier one can also be used with equal comfort and accuracy as this will really depend on the individual using the tool. This can be done by simply gripping the different weighted hammers to feel which one has the most suitable balance for the individual.

• *20 inch hand saw* – although there are a lot of different types of hand saws available in the market for various uses, getting one that will be able to be used for general purposes will be more than enough. This can come in the form of the universal wood saw that has medium sized teeth that are spread out approximately 7 teeth per inch.

• Screwdrivers that come in a set of about 6 pieces will be adequate to handle almost any job. Here too, getting the ones with a rubberized grip would be a better option to look for.

• Tape and a stapler are both tools a kit cannot do without. Although these items may seem simple, they are able to keep almost anything is place either temporarily or permanently.

- A drill with a good variety of bits will facilitate any handyman job very well. Getting both the cordless and the electric drill will be ideal for the handyman who needs the flexibility of both types.
- Level bars are also another essential item, as they are a good measuring gauge to ensure all the fixtures and items are placed in a level and balanced manner.
- *Stanley knife* – this tool is particularly useful when there is a need for a sharp yet safe cutting tool. The safety and storage designs are well done and the size is compatible and comfortable to use.
- *20 mm and 8 mm chisels* - these tools are suitable for most woodwork jobs. However, it is essential to keep these tools sharp at all times to ensure they give optimum results when needed.
- *Junior hack saw* – most D.I.Y. jobs are usually quite small and very rarely complicated, thus the junior hack saw should be able to work well for most sawing related jobs. They also work well on wood and metal, such as cutting metal pipes, trimming window blinds and shortening wood pieces.
- *Punch* – this tool is especially suitable for hammering the heads of nails below the surface of wood prior to filing. It is

considered one of the more essential tools next to the hammer when it comes to jobs involving nails.

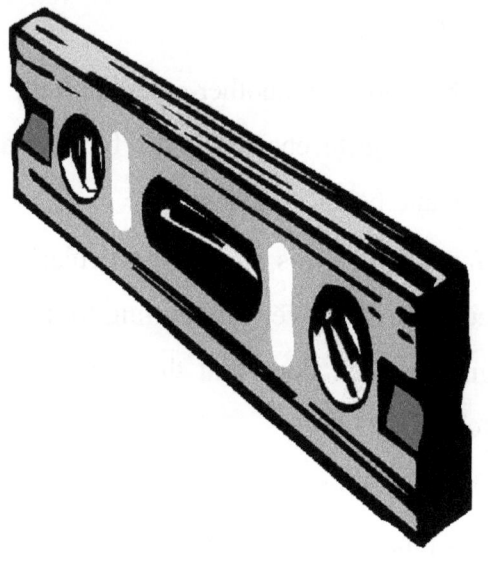

Chapter 2

Top Skills 1: Woodworking

Synopsis

Woodworking can be approached as a hobby or as a profession; either way, working with wood has been an exercise almost everyone has participated in at some point in their lives. With the correct tools and some knowledge, woodworking can be a very fulfilling experience.

Woodworking

Most of the tools that are used for woodworking are sharp and potentially dangerous, therefore care needs to be exercised whenever such tools are being handled. Taking the appropriate precautions will limit the chances of injury. Experienced woodworkers will be able to difference between the various types and qualities of wood and also their most suitable uses. Knowing the advantages and disadvantages of certain woods is helpful to ensure the appropriate choices are made for the particular job at hand.

Having a suitable amount of space to work with is also another point to consider, as limited space will eventually contribute to mistakes and injury occurring frequently. There should be adequate space for the relevant tools to be laid out for use and also space for the assembling of units that may be rather big and bulky. Without such space allowances, getting the job done well will be a challenge which could contribute to a lot of stress.

When it comes to tackling joints for woodworking, the use of nails, screws and other mechanical fasteners, may not be always necessary. In woodwork exercises there are a lot of other types of joineries that can be applied and such methods produce equal quality work.

Woodwork does not always mean working with wood to produce pieces such as furniture, cabinets, frames and other more conventional items. It can also be a form of wood turning which would involve the designing and making of items such as bowls, decorative pots, pens and decorational art effects.

Chapter 3

Top Skills 2: Plumbing

Synopsis

Plumbing can almost always be a rather complicated and difficult task to tackle. Therefore, it may be a better option to hire a professional to get the job done correctly and to ensure a suitably lasting effect.

Plumbing

The expertise of a handyman, when it comes to handling plumbing jobs, includes fixing water leaks in kitchens, bathrooms and any other areas where water is the cause of the problem. For a seemingly simple task like changing a faucet, especially if the faucet chosen is a fancy and more decorative styled piece, hiring a plumber to install the unit maybe better than actually trying to tackle the task without any expert knowledge. In almost all instances, what may seem like a simple and straight forward task to the layman, is actually a rather complicated plumbing issue that would be best handled by a professional handyman with plumbing expertise. This is also the most cost effective and timely way of handling any plumbing problem.

Most basic plumbing tool kits would include the following:

- *Plunger* – this tool should be able to fix most minor blockages without much fuss. It can be used in bathrooms, toilets and kitchens where the blockage is not extensive or serious.
- *Hand auger* – this tool is usually used when the plunger is not able to deal with the blockage adequately. The design of

this tool enables it to be stuffed down into pipes and drains, to unclog any blockages.

- *Wrench set* – these tools help to deal with leaks and loose pipes and the selection should include a basin wrench, a pipe wrench and an adjustable wrench.
- *Tongue and groove pliers* – these tools are also known by their brand, which is Channelocks. This tool is used to tighten, loosen, grab, twist or hold anything related to a plumbing problem.

Chapter 4

Top Skills 3: Basic Electronics

Synopsis

With a little bit of trained knowledge, it is not that difficult to understand the basics of electronics and their connective uses. Having a basic knowledge of how circuitry boards work will help you to have a better picture of the overall electronics experience. All electronics people should know the various connotations involved in this line, before actually attempting to handle any electric related problems.

Basic Electronics

The following are some elements connected to the electronics theme:

- There are basically two types of electrical signals, which are AC and DC. With the DC style, the electricity flows in one direction between the power and the ground where there is always a positive source of voltage and ground source of voltage. The electricity is defined as having a voltage and a current rating which are then depicted as Amps.

- The circuit is a complete and closed path through which the electric current flows between power and ground, thus an open circuit would work in the opposite way of where the flow of electricity is broken.

- The resistance feature is an important part of the circuitry as it ensures the electrical flow is being channeled and used, otherwise a short circuit will occur. Short circuits occurring are bad as they can cause severe damage to the electrical item and also cause fires and explosions. Therefore, ensuring the electrical flow is never wired directly to the ground is very important.

- Understanding and choosing between series and parallel is essential in deciding its appropriateness for the intended electoral item.
- Resistors are in place to help reduce and balance the flow of electricity. They come with different wattage ratings, which are low voltage DC circuits of ¼ watt resistors.
- Capacitors are components that store the electricity and then discharge it into the circuit when there is a disturbance which results in a drop in electricity.
- Diodes are components which are polarized and they only allow electrical current flows in one direction. This is useful when there is a need to check for a flow in the wrong direction.

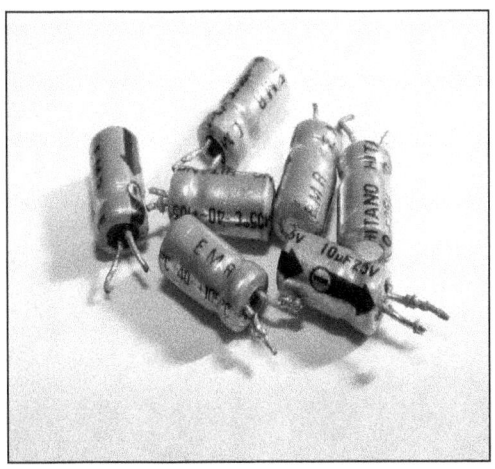

Chapter 5

Top Skills 4: Advanced Electronics

Synopsis

There are several different elements that are usually covered in the advanced electronics platform. Exploring these features will allow anyone to make the appropriate choices for their needs.

Advanced Electronics

The following are some of the areas where advanced electricians are prominently featured for their individualistic contributions:

- *Project definition* – at this point, the idea behind the need for the advanced electrician contributions is decided. Here the various features are matched and chosen.

- *Cost analysis* – the advance electricians tools will be able to provide the relevant assistance for development and identifying new possibilities where advanced electronics can be effective.

- There is also a positive contribution where the advanced electrician will be able to assist in any probable applications for the architecture and design for any product or endeavor.

- *Software development* – advance electronics can also contribute in this area, where the embedded programs can have better hardware installed, which produce more efficient and functional codes for the equipment.

- Advance electronics can also contribute to the products interfacing with computers and where the software functions systematically to ensure the hardware accepts and understands it.

With constant advancment electronics progress, there is always a possibility of new products and inventions being developed. These developments are meant to enhance the general working of everything connected to the comforts of human life. There are a lot of areas where advanced electronics can apply to the common person and these may include hiring the services of a handyman who has such capabilities, to address problems such as home repairs, remodeling and maintenance. Having the services of a handyman, who is well versed with the advanced electronics platform, will help to ensure all problems are accurately and effectively solved.

Chapter 6

Working On Floors, Walls & Ceilings

Synopsis

Most people today opt to do their own home improvement work and although such exercises require a certain amount of experience, the internet is a great source and encouragement for those who want to tackle these improvements themselves.

Helpful Hints

The following are some tips on how this can be done systematically and without causing too much stress:

- *Floors* – lay out the band boards by using the square, tape measure and pencil and then the task of measuring and marking can begin. Set measurements have to be followed to ensure the finished work is well placed and there are no unsightly overlaps. Cutting the floor joist according to the subtraction of 3 inches for the band boards should be done. The attaching of the joists to band boards should be done with the use of 16 penny nails. Then a bead of adhesive caulk could be applied down each joist using an instrument called a caulk gun. The subflooring should be laid out carefully, ensuring the long edge lays perpendicular to the way the studs run. The 8 penny nails should be spaced every 8 – 10 inches down each stud.

- *Walls* – very similar to the out laying of floors with the exception of remembering to mark out allowances for windows and doors and other walls that may tie in. Cutting wall studs, headers, jack studs, sill plates, crown or king studs, partition posts and corner posts, should be done to the required length. Measurements should also be done up the length of the wall and across the base of the wall. Erect the wall and attach it to the floor suing 16 penny nails through the bottom plate and into the floor joists.

- *Ceilings* – this is similar to the laying of the ceiling and requires the nailing of the ceiling joists at an angle to the wall without splitting the floor joist. Then attach the ceiling joist hangers to the ceiling joist and top plate of the walls ideally using joists hanger nails.

Chapter 7

Working On Windows, Doors & Lighting

Synopsis

The task of working on windows, the D.I.Y. style, requires a few tools and some simple step that are fairly easy to follow.

How To Do It Yourself

The first step would be to get the precise measurement noted down in order to purchase the material needed accordingly. Testing the fit of the new unit would be wise, before actually installing it permanently. A polyurethane sealant is applied around the existing window frame to ensure it is weather proof, then installation screws are used to fasten it into the solid wood frame. Put in the window, bottom first, and then tilt the top into place, then use thin wedges called shims to center the window.

As for doors, the first step involves measuring the doorway opening and then laying the door on sawhorses. Remember to provide in the measurements an inch or two for carpets to run under the door. Then, apply painter's tape along the length of the marked out frame and on the plate of the saw, while cutting the door along the mark. Screw the hinges and the door together, then move it through the frame. Once the door is leveled out, nail through the frame to the wall then use low expansion foam to fill the spaces between the door and the wall which should effectively keep the door in place.

As for lighting, the first thing would be to disconnect the power supply which can be done by turning off the circuit breaker or removing the fuse. Remove any coverings and the light bulbs and then disconnect them from the electrical box by removing the screws. Observe the existing connections before replacing them with new ones so that the job can be simply mimicked. The 3 wires are white – negative, black – positive and the green or bare copper – ground wires. The black wire should be connected to the brass screw, the white to the silver screw and green to the green screw. Then remount the fixture and turn the power on.

Chapter 8

Working On Bathrooms, Kitchens & Basements

Synopsis

Working on D.I.Y. projects can be very rewarding if the individual is well equipped mentally and physically. Therefore, before actually attempting the jobs, one should be fully prepared in these areas.

Be Well Equipped!

There are several different areas that are to be considered when looking into remodeling a bathroom, and these would include bathroom accessories, bathroom countertops, bathroom designs, bathroom flooring and installations, bathroom planning and remodeling, bathroom sinks, bathroom toilet, bathroom walls, ceramic wall tiling, bathroom cabinets, bathroom decorations, bathroom fixtures, bathroom shower and a bathroom vanity. Each area requires a different set of actions and perhaps a variety of tools to get the job done efficiently and accurately. Therefore, some careful attention and knowledge should be exercised.

The D.I.Y. kitchen project also requires attention in several different areas and this would ideally include building the cabinets, designing the kitchen space and planning out where each item fits in such as the, kitchen countertops, kitchen plumbing, kitchen decor and kitchen safety items. However, there are simple smaller changes that can be made that may bring about a whole new pleasant look and feel. These may include, simply changing the counter tops, flooring, painting the kitchen or replacing the cabinets, all of which are a much cheaper alternative than actually attempting to change the whole kitchen.

Basements are a little tricky to attempt to do yourself, but none the less, it can still be done with attention given to certain important areas. Ensuring the project only begins when the area is completely dry is very important. Then checking the electrical coding and ensuring it is done accordingly should be the next step. Hammering nails in is ok to get the job done but using a tool called a shotgun is better for this kind of construction. Include furring in ½ inch measurements between the inner and outer walls. Include polyurethane sheeting to keep the moisture from seeping in and also consider insulation that is completely enclosed in a vapor barrier.

Chapter 9

Working On The House Exterior

Synopsis

Choosing a suitable style for the exterior of the home when a remodeling project is needed should involve a few important considerations. These would be elements such as, deciding whether the idea is to stick out and be different or to blend in with only a few minor features that are attention grabbing.

Making Your Home Beautiful

As there are several different styles to consider, having some knowledge about the various designs and what it entails would be a good place to start. The following are some simple outlines on the more popular designs used:

- **Farmhouse** – here the main facade feature would be the covered porch that usually stretches along the front and goes around the sides of the unit. One may also consider the steep gable roof, shutters and horizontal siding that make up the style of the farmhouse.

- **Georgian** – the symmetrical design evident here comes from the stately brick facade that amplifies the Georgian style. The decorative keystones over the shuttered windows, the columned entryway and the gabled dormers all add to the distinct characteristic of this style.

- **Cape Cod** – the simple lines used here contribute to the symmetrical design, where the dormers and the dominant roofline dictate its distinctness. The roofline, which typically extends down to the first floor, is what makes this design mirror the early styles.

- **Victorian** – Victorian style architecture has a very distinctive style that is recognizable in the home corner turret, its wraparound porch and the ornate detailing work. This is also another style that is considered dated, yet still charmingly drawing the interest of a lot of home owners.

- **Mediterranean** – the arched windows and stucco exterior are all part of this particular style. Adding to this, the low pitched tiled roof is an excellent example of the Mediterranean style.

- **Contemporary** – then there is the ever popular more suburban look which is displayed through its asymmetrical design of varied rooflines, stark facade and hold windows. In some designs, there is the add-on of a circular tower with a domed skylight.

Chapter 10

Protect Yourself From Injuries

Synopsis

Injuries are a common occurrence when dealing with handyman work. However, some measure can be taken to minimize the injuries and its frequency.

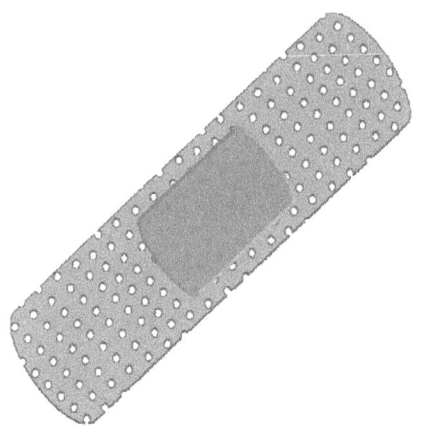

Stay Safe!

The following are some of the areas where caution should be extended to help minimize the possibility of injuries:

- The handyman should always try to avoid using the table saw fence for crosscuts. This is especially so when making the mistake of starting on wood that is still wet or a bowed and twisted piece of lumber. Using a fence as a guide for cross cutting is dangerous and a better alternative would be to use a miter gauge or build a cross cutting sled.

- Removing the blade guard is another action that should not be practiced, although a lot of handymen seem to disregard this very important precaution. Failing to observe this will certainly result in injury, should any distractions occur while using the blade.

- Holding the board with the hands directly behind the circular saw, is also a folly often taken for granted. Using a temporary nail or clamp is a much safer option.

- Placing the hands or using the hand to grip near the area where nail guns are about to be used is also another mistake that is often made. The hand position holding the board should not be too close to the nail gun. Handling nail guns carefully is very important, as a lot of accidents occur with careless misuse. Disconnecting the hose and keeping away from the trigger is very important.

- Careless use of knives or blades is also another common cause of injury. Therefore, when using either of these, the handyman should keep focused and not allow any distractions to complicate an already potentially dangerous situation.

- Using the relevant protective gear for the face and eye area is important. Safety goggles and face shield should be a standard piece of protective wear used by the handyman.

Chapter 11

Always Have A First Aid Kit

Synopsis

As with everything, the measure of safety should always be taken into consideration. Both indoors and outdoors, there should always be some assistance available when medical problems or accidents occur and having a complete first aid kit is something that is considered important.

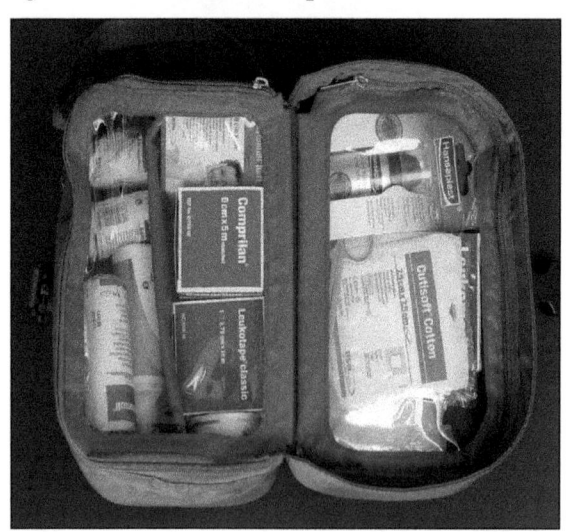

Be Safe

A well-stocked first aid kit is sometime the only recourse an individual has to the first line of defense when accidents occur at home, at work or outdoors. In most cases, it is a very good source to turn to when there is a medical emergency and actual medical assistance is not available or close at hand. However, a first aid kit should be well equipped at all times and updated periodically as most of the contents have an expiration date. An ill equipped first aid kit will be of no use to anyone.

The following are some of the items that should ideally be part of a complete first aid kit – first aid manual, sterile gauze pads of different sizes, adhesive tape, adhesive bandages in several sizes, elastic bandages, a splint, antiseptic wipes, soap, antibiotic ointment, antiseptic solutions, hydrocortisone cream, acetaminophen and ibuprofen, extra prescription medications that can be used without a doctor's prescription, tweezers, sharp scissors, safety pins, disposable instant cold packs, calamine lotion, alcohol wipes or ethyl alcohol, a thermometer, a couple of pairs of plastic non latex gloves, a flash light and extra batteries and maybe a blanket.

Although some of the items listed may seem a little extreme, it would still be prudent to include them as being prepared is better than being caught off guard when it comes to being faced with having to handle an emergency situation. Storing the first aid kits in places that are out of the reach of children is another important consideration.

Wrapping Up

You can tackle just about any project around the house by yourself. You just need to make sure that you are first well equipped as well as prepared for the task at hand. Seek out as much information on your project as possible, after all a little help never hurt anyone. Enjoy the sense of pride you get from doing something with your own hard work and two hands. So why keep paying others to do your handy work who are likely doing a poor job? Get out there and do it yourself, I know you can! I hope this book has provided you with some useful information. Good luck on your future projects!

www.ingramcontent.com/pod-product-compliance
Ingram Content Group UK Ltd.
Pitfield, Milton Keynes, MK11 3LW, UK
UKHW020645060526
12295UKWH00012B/173